Combining two great hobbies in your backyard

Garden railroading combines two seemingly separate hobbies—gardening and model railroading—and blends them in concert to create a miniature world in the backyard. This blending can have the positive effect of involving more than one person in the project, as garden railroading often involves the entire family.

Garden railroading can involve the talents and interests of the whole family. Starting out is easy, and both your garden and railroad can grow as time, money, and space permit. Photo by William Zuback

Life partners sometimes become a major influence on the direction a garden railroad takes. When my wife first saw the railroad in the backyard, she said, "Cool! I can put my toys out here!" She's since convinced me that we really do need a pond, and that we also need to run a spur to the vegetable garden.

Children also enjoy being involved. I'm a second-generation garden railroader myself, having grown up around the hobby in the 1970s.

The appeal of garden railroading, however, stems not so much from the models themselves, but from their environment. Outdoors, you deal with nature. Everything is real. This does bring the occasional hazard in the form of wild animals, errant soccer balls, fallen leaves, and even tree branches, but this also is part of the inherent charm of a garden railroad.

As someone once said, "The difference between indoor and outdoor model railroading can be summed up rather simply: Inside, you spend your time carefully placing small weeds between the rails. Outside, you spend your time removing them."

The renaissance

Running model trains outdoors seems to many to be a new and exciting facet of model railroading. Certainly in the past 15 years, garden railroading has become one of the fastest growing areas of interest. Its roots, however, go back many years. The practice of running model trains outdoors originated in the late 1800s in England and enjoyed some popularity in the United States in the early part of the 20th century. But by the 1940s, it had almost disappeared.

It wasn't until 1968 that the pieces fell into place for garden railroading to begin its renaissance. That's the year Ernst Paul Lehmann, a German toy manufacturer, began producing the LGB brand of model trains designed to be run outdoors. Its early offerings were based on European meter gauge equipment, but a few years later, LGB started to offer models of U.S. prototypes. With that, the die was cast, and the garden railroading hobby was off to a slow, but sure, start.

In the 30 years since garden railroading began to flourish in the United States, there has been a great deal of diversification of modeling interests. Manufacturers have been quick to follow up on that broadening audience with a wide array of products.

One gauge, many scales

The one common factor for garden railroads is the No. 1 track gauge, with rails 45mm (1¾") apart. Models in many different scales operate on that track gauge, and many garden railroaders don't mind mixing these scales.

LGB started with No. 1 gauge track and figured out that to represent meter gauge prototypes, the proportion of prototype to model should be 1:22.5. LGB has remained active in the garden railroad field and offers an extensive line of 1:22.5 models. While its models often lack the scale fidelity offered by other manufacturers, they have maintained their reputation for robustness and innovation. Many LGB models are highly sought after by collectors—an attribute that has evaded most other models.

Careful attention to details, such as placement of the model animals on this farm, can add much to the overall scene. Photo by Michael Soliday

To represent 3-foot gauge, which was the most common narrow gauge track used in the United States, modelers here soon figured out that the correct proportion should be 1:20.3, which means the models are about 10 percent larger than those made to 1:22.5 meter gauge proportion.

Bachmann has a line of 1:20.3 locomotives that has helped raise the standard against which other models are measured. A few companies offer brass locomotives in this scale, and there are a number of car kits available, too.

To use No. 1 gauge track to represent standard gauge, the correct proportion is 1:32, or ⅜" to the foot. Märklin offers models in this scale.

Three diesels lead the morning freight through Johnstown on the CST&J Railroad in Ohio. Photo by Marc Horovitz

Aristo-Craft and USA Trains have emerged as the two largest players for standard gauge models in the garden. Both companies offer high-quality plastic models of some of the most popular modern prototypes. Their chosen scale of 1:29 is not 100 percent accurate, but modelers seem to be forgiving of that discrepancy. LGB also offers a few standard gauge models in 1:26 proportion.

Choice of power

Perhaps one of the most exciting things about modeling outdoors is that you have choices in how you power your trains. Most trains are powered in the traditional "through the rails" method. There are also Digital Command Control (DCC) systems specifically designed for large scale.

When you're outside, however, keeping the track clean and clear of debris gets to be somewhat of a chore. Many people have converted to battery power and radio control. Since the batteries that supply the power are onboard the locomotive, there's no electricity going through the rails. Wiring problems associated with running multiple trains on the same track are eliminated with this method of power. The trade-off is that your locomotives sometimes will have to be "retired" to the enginehouse to have their batteries recharged.

If you want the ultimate railroad realism, you can opt for live steam locomotives. You light a fire in the firebox (using butane or alcohol), which heats water in the boiler. When the steam pressure rises, you open the throttle and start down the line. Many of these locomotives are realistic scale models, while others can get quite whimsical, often bordering on pure fantasy.

From reality to fantasy

The range—from reality to fantasy—makes garden railroading unique. In the garden, you can create your own reality. The climate, rocks, plants, and landscaping form the palette from which you work. The result is a railroad as individual as its creator.

In a great garden railroad, everything works in concert. The trains complement the garden, and vice versa. Garden railroading often finds itself at the opposite end of the prototypical spectrum from indoor modeling. It's not a function of just how "prototypical" a scene is, for a garden railroad is its own prototype—a true original.

Some gardens become miniature reflections of the larger world. Realistically scaled trains flourish in these scenes, doing their part to complete the picture. Other gardens set their own versions of reality. Fantasy runs rampant here, and the creativity of the builder is reflected in colorful trains running through whimsical settings.

Whichever you choose, a garden railroad interacts with the viewer—the smells and sounds call on the mind to open itself up to the garden's world. The trains exist as vehicles—a means for all involved to be transported through this new reality. That is the charm of garden railroading. It's a journey through an ever-changing world, a world that we create and set in motion.

—Kevin Strong

Choosing the right track

Before you put down any track, remember one thing: gauge—the distance between the rails. For us, that would be 45mm, or gauge 1. If you remember that distance, the rest is easy. Stray from this, even by so much as a millimeter, and you're asking for trouble. The rails must be the same distance apart over the entire line. With this one constant in mind, take a look at the variables associated with putting down track in the backyard.

Good trackwork is the key to a bright future for your garden railroad. It's easy to achieve with the wide array of products available for today's modelers. Shown here is handlaid track on Marc Horovitz's Ogden Botanical Railway. Photo by Kevin Strong

The first choice in the track department is whether to use sectional track or flextrack. As the name implies, sectional track comes in sections, or preformed pieces. The variety of pieces has increased considerably in recent years. You can choose from curve radii as tight as 2 feet to as broad as 10 feet. (The radius of a curve is the distance from the midline of the track—halfway between the rails—to the center of the circle of which it is a part. The diameter of the curve is the distance across the complete circle—twice the radius. Be careful not to confuse the two measurements.) Straight track also comes in an ever-increasing variety of lengths.

The greatest advantage of sectional track is its predictability. This means it's easy to draw a plan using sectional track because you know what radii of curves and what lengths of straight track you have to work with. Plans drawn for sectional track translate easily from paper to the garden. You can make out a grocery list of the sections you need, head to the local hobby shop, and buy exactly what you need to build your railroad.

Even though the palette of track sections has increased, you may want more flexibility in planning your garden railroad. That's where the benefits of flextrack come into play. "Flex" is the key word. You can bend flextrack to fit whatever radius you need and can vary that radius infinitely to fit the lines of the garden.

But that is not where the "flexible" options end. With flextrack, you must choose which rail size to use, as well as the size and spacing of the ties on the plastic strips into which you place the rail. You also have a wider

There are three types of track available for the garden. Sectional track (left) is perhaps the easiest to use. Flextrack (center) offers flexibility in planning and track design. Handlaid track (right) offers the highest level of realism but requires the most planning and work. Photo by Kevin Strong

Rail comes in different sizes. Code 332 (left) is the most common rail size for sectional track and stands .332" tall. Code 250 rail (middle, .250" tall) is a common size for flextrack and handlaid track. Code 197 (right, .197" tall) is the most realistic height for rail, but might be too small for reliable use outdoors by beginning modelers. Photo by Kevin Strong

choice of rail material than with sectional track. There is no real cost difference between sectional track and flextrack, given the same rail and tie materials. Cheaper materials can lower your cost per foot, but in the garden, price shouldn't be the only consideration. Laying flextrack requires a bit more planning and work, but the end visual result can be worth it.

A third option is handlaying your own track. You have the same benefit of the choice of rail materials that you have with flextrack, but you can cut the ties to suit your needs. For the beginning garden railroader, however, it's probably better to use either flextrack or sectional track, as they're both quicker and easier. You can always go back later and relay or add handlaid track.

Different rail sizes and materials are available for use in the garden. Rail size is measured in "codes." The code is simply the height of the rail in thousandths of an inch. Code 250 rail stands .250" tall. Most commercially available sectional track is code 332.

If you plan on using commercial switches (known as "turnouts"), then you will have to use code 332 rail to match the switches or buy special rail clamps that will connect the dissimilar sizes. You can buy switches made with smaller-profile rail, but they tend to be a bit more expensive. Conversely, there is no sectional track available in the smaller rail sizes, so you will have to go with flextrack if you wish to use anything other than code 332 rail.

The reasons for using the smaller rail are largely aesthetic. Code 332 rail generally is considered too large to be prototypical. A smaller rail size looks more realistic in the garden. The trade-off is that the smaller rail is not as strong. It doesn't stand up as well to abuse from the elements or errant feet. Many outstanding railroads have been built using code 332 rail, so don't feel like you need to use smaller rail to have a "great" garden railroad. It just isn't the case.

The choice of rail material has as much, if not more, importance as size in the garden setting. Typical choices for rail material include brass, nickel silver, aluminum, steel, and stainless steel. Brass is the most common material. It's easy to work with and solder, and is the material of choice for most sectional track. Some manufacturers offer stainless-steel sectional track as well. It requires little cleaning but is difficult to cut and work with for custom trackwork. Nickel silver is similar in properties to brass but has the advantage of a more realistic color. My experience with nickel silver rail in the indoor scales indicates similar maintenance requirements to brass, including frequency of cleaning.

Steel rail is also an option, but it rusts just like the real thing. In damp climates, the rail will rust to the point of absolute uselessness within one or two seasons.

Aluminum rail is the cheapest of all available materials. Price, however, is its only real advantage. It's the weakest of all the metals, and is prone to bending and kinking, even though it's easy to cut and shape. Aluminum is also an inconsistent conductor of electricity. Although it's a conductive metal, trouble arises in getting the electrons to flow, due to oxidation between the rail sections. Aluminum can't be soldered, so any electrical connections have to be mechanical, made with either aluminum or stainless-steel fasteners. Brass, copper, and other common metals will react when in contact with aluminum, the result being that both metals corrode and the connection breaks.

I recommend using aluminum only if you're planning on building a live-steam or battery-powered railroad. If you're going to use track power, I'd recommend the added expense of either brass or nickel-silver rail.

If you opt for flextrack, the first thing you'll need is a rail bender, as seen at right. Most track manufacturers offer them. A rail bender is the best way to get smooth, even curves, especially when you want to bend rail to tighter radii. You don't need to bend the curves to the exact radius; you will be able to finesse them when you actually set the track down in the garden.

Whether you use flex or sectional track, you will need a

Soldered rail joints, such as on this brass track, offer the most reliable electrical connection. Photo by Kevin Strong

A rail bender is used to pre-curve rail for flextrack. Photo by Kevin Strong

Rail clamps offer strong connections with a degree of flexibility in design. These clamps, from Richard Hillman, are insulated, allowing for electrical isolation of an industrial spur. Photo by Kevin Strong

Screws through the rail joiners are perhaps the simplest method of maintaining a good connection between the rails. Photo by Kevin Strong

way of fastening the track together to maintain electrical continuity throughout (if you're using track power). If you think you can rely solely on the rail joiners that come with the track, you're asking for trouble down the line.

There are three basic ways of making sure the track connections are good and solid. The first is to solder each joint, ensuring a good electrical connection. While this method provides almost bulletproof electrical continuity, it has its drawbacks. To start, there's the heat element. You'll need either a very large soldering iron or a small torch to heat the rail enough for the solder to flow. This can melt nearby ties if you're not careful. Second, soldering is nearly permanent. You'll have to unsolder joints to make changes. Also, you'll have to allow for expansion and contraction by using unsoldered joints every so often. (These joints should each have a jumper wire soldered across them.)

The other popular method is to use rail clamps. These replace the rail joiners, clamping the rails together. This isn't a cheap method, but clamps can be removed easily to accommodate future changes or expansion. Special clamps are available that enable you to join two sizes of rail, and insulated rail clamps allow you to create electrically isolated sidings where you can park trains. Rail clamps offer a great deal of strength that you don't get with regular rail joiners.

A cheap alternative to rail clamps is to add a screw through a slide-on rail joiner. Aristo-Craft and USA Trains use this feature in their track. Each rail section is predrilled and tapped for a small machine screw. If you're not using track from those manufacturers, the same thing can be accomplished by drilling holes through the web of the rail joiner and using small self-tapping screws to hold everything together.

Garden railroaders have many options when it comes to putting down track in the garden. The key isn't so much what you use, but *how* you use it. You need to decide what you want and how much work you're willing to do. With solid roadbed and well-assembled track, there's no reason your railroad won't be able to provide years of reliable operation.

—Kevin Strong

Thinking beyond that first shovelful

There's one constant among garden railroaders when it comes to building their railroads—all will build their next railroads differently. That's something that's been stated and restated by beginning and seasoned garden railroaders alike.

I recently had the opportunity to do just that—start over. A couple of years ago, I left the frozen tundra of western New York for the warmer and significantly sunnier expanses of Denver, Colorado. In doing so, five years of labor, including the previous summer's addition of a large pond, stayed behind. This move, and the ensuing search for a house with a suitable backyard, got me thinking about what elements are important in planning a garden railroad. Most of these have nothing to do with the actual railroad, but rather how I intend to interact with it and make it as convenient as possible.

When looking back on my old railroad, the one thing I realized was that I didn't run trains as often as I would have liked. The primary reason for this perhaps lay in the time needed to physically get the trains outside. I stored models on shelves in the basement and hand-carried each car out to the railroad, two or three at a time. Prototypical operations in the garden generally required five or six trips up and down the stairs each time I wanted to play.

This time, the trains will be kept closer to the railroad. There are a few ways to accomplish this. One of the most common methods is to run tracks into a nearby shed or garage. Other people have built lean-tos or other enclosed storage cases along fences or otherwise unseen parts of the railroad. A third option is to run the trains into the house through a hole in a wall. These methods eliminate the need to handle rolling stock prior to each run.

Rock cuts lend a sense of depth and drama to a miniature landscape. The key is to make sure you can easily reach into the cut to remove leaves, twigs, and derailed equipment. Photo by Kevin Strong

If running tracks into a storage structure isn't possible, consider running them as close as possible to where the trains will be stored to minimize carrying distances. Not having to carry trains up and down flights of stairs is definitely an advantage.

Of course, getting the trains to the railroad is only half the battle. Getting them onto the track can be equally challenging. Adequate access to all points of the railroad is very important. Dry riverbeds and miniature roadways are some of the most common methods of gaining access, but the entire railroad can't be a dry riverbed. Places to put your feet are especially important around switches and other features that require frequent attention. Strategically placed stones can go a long way toward providing such access. One of my favorite methods of placing such stones is to have a pile of them lying around

Jim Strong watches as a Woodland Railway passenger train eases down the grade from Hemlock Hills. Formal paths, such as the one at left, wend around the outside of the entire railroad, while more informal paths allow access into the railway itself. Photo by Kevin Strong

A flagstone path gives operators easy access to the complex switchwork at Woodland Junction on the Woodland Railway. Photo by Kevin Strong

when I run trains. Anywhere I find myself needing to step, I grab a stone and place it there. I worry later about how best to landscape the stones into the surrounding terrain—the important thing is to get them there as placeholders.

Access to tunnels is also important. Tunnels should be no longer than twice the length of your arm, for what should be obvious reasons. Tunnels are great places for a variety of wildlife to congregate, and trains will derail in the middle as a result. At the same time, make sure you can physically access the tunnel's entrance in order to reach in. There's one tunnel on my dad's Woodland Railway that requires a bit of a contortionist's act to reach into. Yes, we've lost trains in there. No, they didn't emerge from the tunnel unscathed after being poked out with a broom handle.

Of course, if you can't go to the mountain, the solution may be to bring the mountain to you. Elevated railways offer ease of access without the problems inherent in ground-level lines. When everything is within arm's reach, there's less need for other access features, except for routine maintenance chores such as weeding and cleaning track. The drawback is that elevated lines initially require more work to raise the ground to a high enough level.

There are many different ways of elevating a railroad. Most common methods involve bringing in large quantities of dirt or other fill material to gain the needed elevation. The roadbed and track can be built up first, then back-filled, or you can bring in the dirt and do the landscaping before the track is laid. Regardless, you'll want to build some kind of retaining wall so the dirt doesn't eventually wash away.

You have many choices of materials for these walls. Landscaping blocks, timbers, and railroad ties are the most common materials used. Natural stone can be more expensive, but the improved aesthetics usually make the expense worth the effort. If you're fortunate to live in a particularly mountainous or rocky area, the materials may be right at your fingertips.

Shrubbery can make an effective virtual retaining wall. Here, the track has to be supported by some kind of substructure. The vegetation grows up around the support, giving the track the appearance of running along the tops of the bushes. This method works well along fences and other areas where building a real retaining wall would otherwise block groundwater drainage.

An important consideration that so many garden railroaders overlook when building railroads is the future. They design their railroads looking perhaps 3 or 4 years ahead. Seldom do they look 15 or 20 years down the line to what might happen.

The greatest consideration is the possibility of a relocation. Can the railroad exist as a garden in its own right, without the track? A young family bought my old house, and the young boys fell in love with the railroad. I don't know how well my old line would have worked as just a rock garden. One thing I've learned from my current house hunt is that people have strange ideas about what makes "good" landscaping. I can only imagine what prospective buyers thought when they saw my backyard.

The other long-term consideration is the addition or subtraction of family members. Our next yard has to be large enough to accommodate both the railroad and the future addition of little ones, be they human or furry. Kids and pets need room to run and play, so the railroad should be constructed appropriately if all are to peacefully coexist. Elevating the railroad minimizes the damaging effects of soccer balls, puppy paws, and crawling kids. If you're planning to install a water feature, it may be a good idea to elevate that as well, to keep children from accidentally falling in or to keep curious four-legged friends at least partially at bay. I know my previous next-door neighbor's dog enjoyed afternoon drinks from her new "water bowl."

Raccoons, deer, and other wildlife are equally attracted to garden ponds and have a tendency to be clumsy around things such as train tracks, miniature plants, and buildings. The important thing here is balance. You want to raise the railroad high enough to keep it and others out of harm's way, but at the same time, you want to allow the little ones the chance to be able to enjoy the trains. That was always my biggest problem growing up with the indoor scales—what the builders saw as "eye level" wasn't what I saw at eye level. Garden railroads are best enjoyed while sitting in a chair, not standing on one.

Paths don't need to be long, or even noticeable. Here, a few well-placed rocks provide needed access to the railway without calling attention to themselves. Photo by Kevin Strong

These are just some of the thoughts that have been running through my mind as I begin to consider building the "next" garden railroad. While I have every intention of building this one to last a bit longer than just 5 years, nobody can predict the future. Many of us simply don't have the luxury of staying in one house for 30-plus years.

When we design our railroads, we need to keep the inevitability of change in mind. We need to build our lines to accommodate what lies in the future. At the same time, we need to remember that our railroads should be enjoyed in the here-and-now.

—Kevin Strong

Mike and Jeanie Harris used railroad ties and landscaping blocks to create a terraced garden area out of the sloping back edge of their yard. The terracing gives a formal boundary to the railway, while elevating it to a workable height. Photo by Kevin Strong

The right plant in the right place

To a novice gardener, the topic of plant-hardiness zones can be as confusing as gauge and scale terminology is to the beginning model railroader. If you want your plants to survive and thrive, it's important to identify your hardiness zone and stick with planting recommendations for your specific climate.

The USDA North American Hardiness Zone Map is one of the most widely used and recognized plant-zone rating systems. Plants are designated by their ability to survive the coldest temperatures. In 2000, the Department of Agriculture updated its cold-hardiness map, showing the lowest temperatures expected in all regions of North America.

It includes 11 zones, ranging from Zone 1 (the coldest, beginning at -50 degrees F) to Zone 11 (the warmest, with low temperatures expected above 40 degrees F). The first 10 zones are broken into two sub-zones (a, b) of 5-degree increments, narrowing the delineation more precisely.

To use this system, simply go to the Web site listed above and click on the map. It will take you closer to your area with color-coded zones.

—Pat Hayward

The USDA Plant Hardiness Zone Map: www.usna.usda.gov/Hardzone/index.html

The most-versatile plants for garden railway trees

Can you imagine your hometown with few or no trees? Think of the sun beating down on you month after month, heat reflecting off the streets and sidewalks, baking the lawns and gardens. Or imagine orchards with no fruit trees, yards with no colorful fall leaves, or children with no tire swings. Garden railways' towns and farms need trees, too. Here are 10 of the best for all-around beauty, scale appropriateness, and ease of maintenance.

1. In warmer climates, **snow roses** (*Serissa foetida*) are probably the most versatile, attractive, and in-scale trees for landscaping cities, towns, and farms. Left to their own devices, these tiny evergreen flowering trees will stay under 2 feet tall and wide. Trimmed, they can be kept small. The leathery, dark-green leaves are narrow and less than an inch long, and the trees often are covered with miniature blossoms of white, pink, or rose.

Because everything about this plant is in scale, it gives an immediate sense of reality to miniature scenes and vignettes. Many varieties are available, especially from specialty miniature-plant growers. One of my favorite uses of snow roses is at Miniland, at Legoland in Carlsbad, California, where snow roses represent the flowering cherry trees of Washington, D.C., in the springtime. Snow roses are tropical plants, so they cannot tolerate frost. Garden railroaders in colder climates can bring their plants indoors for the winter.

2. Miniature Chinese elms (*Ulmus parvifolia* cultivars) are another incredibly useful group of trees, especially for garden railways in Zones 6-9. True elms, their tiny leaves and dark bark are perfectly in scale for landscaping town squares and roadways. 'Hokkaido' is the tiniest of all, with leaves less than 1½ inches long and very compact growth. Hokkaido is particularly attractive because it forms a corky bark even when quite young, and needs little care to stay small and tidy.

Next in scale is 'Seiju,' which is a little easier to find and a lot less expensive. It also grows faster. Seiju leaves are slightly

Hard-working farmhands catch up on the local news under the welcome shade of a Cherry Blossom snow rose in full bloom. A quick pruning twice a month during the growing season is all that's necessary to maintain these lovely trees in the Serussa Springs Railway of Ross and Sue Piper of Lakeside, California. Photo by Sue Piper

A red laceleaf Japanese maple shades the station in The Great Western Reserve Railroad of Don and Gayle Oeters of Cincinnati, Ohio. Photo by Pat Hayward

A green laceleaf Japanese maple offers shade to downtown shoppers on the RCK Railroad of Ralph and Kristine Davy in Lansing, Illinois. This maple's finely dissected leaves give the appearance of a smaller-scale tree. Photo by Pat Hayward

This young Strieb's Findling cotoneaster will soon be producing fruit on Ed and Joanne Frey's Columbine & Larkspur Railway in Loveland, Colorado. Photo by Pat Hayward

larger than Hokkaido. With regular pruning and trimming, Seiju can be wonderful additions to rural roadsides and as shade trees for homesteads. Left to grow a bit more naturally, they make excellent intermediate trees for areas away from finescale details. For garden railroaders in slightly colder climates, the hybrid 'Jacqueline Hillier' grows well, although it does tend to grow rather vigorously at times.

3. Dwarf and laceleaf Japanese maples (*Acer palmatum* cultivars) are staple trees for many garden railroaders. The naturally dwarf varieties, such as 'Sharp's Pygmy' and 'Beni hime,' are excellent choices for their compact growth habit and miniature leaves. Unfortunately, they can be hard to find and are a bit expensive.

Standard varieties of Japanese maple require more shaping and controlling to stay small, but they are readily available and won't empty your wallet if you need more than one. Some people find the laceleaf (*Acer palmatum dissectum*) varieties a nice compromise because their finely dissected leaves give the appearance of being smaller scale, and their natural growth habit is mounding.

One of my favorite maples is trident maple (*Acer buergerianum*), which has a slightly larger, three-pointed leaf. It needs regular pruning, but "trunks up" quickly and has a stately appearance. There's also a miniature trident maple, 'Mino yatsubusa,' which looks promising. Most maples are hardy in Zones 5-9.

4. Common myrtle (*Myrtus communis*) really is "common" because it's a wonderful evergreen hedging plant in warmer climates (Zones 8-9). Dwarf myrtle (*Myrtus communis* 'Compacta') is slightly less common, but still is available for small hedges and edging.

Because of its tiny leaves, compact growth habit, and ease of shearing, dwarf myrtle can be used in the railway for several purposes. Left to grow bushy and full, rows of dwarf myrtle can delineate backyard boundaries, line parkways, or provide living "view breaks" for passing trains. They also can be trimmed into small-scale ornamental trees for many landscape purposes.

5. Cotoneaster (pronounced kuh-TOE-knee-ast-er) are commonly found woody groundcovers and small shrubs. They produce dainty white blossoms (just like apple trees) that mature and ripen to form tiny red fruits. Several varieties are useful, including thyme-leaf (*C. microphyllus* 'Thymifolia') and *C. dammeri* 'Strieb's Findling.' They are hardy in Zones 4-9.

6. Dwarf and miniature birches are great options for railroaders in colder climates, and several nice ones are available for consideration. 'Trost's Dwarf' (*Betula pendula* 'Trost's Dwarf') is my favorite for urban landscapes because its lacy, light-green foliage and weeping habit fit well into most neighborhood scenes. Bog birch, *Betula nana* (*nana* means "small"), is a North American native shrubby birch at high altitudes (Zone 3) and has tiny, rounded leaves. This is a real gem that can be worked up into a tree with a little care.

I've recently heard about a new dwarf river birch named Little King (*Betula nigra* 'Little King') that has interesting cinnamon/salmon-colored peeling bark like the species. It's a good choice for bonsai, so it can stay the right size with pruning. Most of the birches tolerate moderate to wet conditions and are hardy in Zones 4-10, possibly colder.

7. **Boxwood** is a familiar tree, and the dwarf and miniature forms really are fine because they have small, rounded leaves, are evergreen and easy to grow, can be easily trimmed, and are hardy in a wide range of temperatures (Zones 5-9). Most varieties of English boxwood (*Buxus sempervirens*) are fine and relatively inexpensive, but for the most compact trees, look for *B. microphylla* 'Kingsville Dwarf' and 'Morris Midget.'

8. Gardeners in colder areas know the **New Zealand tea tree** (*Leptospermum scoparium*) as a florist's item, but it makes a lovely flowering ornamental tree for railways in warmer climates (Zones 8-10). Tea trees have small, rounded leaves that measure about ½" long, and produce small, ½"-wide flowers in shades of pink, rose, and white. They bloom most heavily during late spring and early summer but can produce blossoms periodically throughout the season. Keep them pruned, and you'll be pleased with the effects.

9. **Miniature andromeda** or **little heath trees** (*Pieris japonica* cultivars) are popular in full-size landscapes for the same reason we like them in garden railroads: Their glossy, bronzy-green foliage is evergreen; they produce clusters of fragrant, bell-shaped flowers in spring; they're easy to grow; and, best of all, they're resistant to deer browsing. Several dwarf varieties are available, but I recommend 'Little Heath' because the leaves are also quite small. Pieris prefer slightly acid soil and are hardy in Zones 6-8.

Nathaniel pauses to enjoy the springtime spectacle of these New Zealand tea trees. These trees are slow growers and are resistant to garden pests. Also important, they thrive in full sun or partial shade. Snow White is blooming on the left and Aurora Nana Rosea on the right. Photo by Sue Piper

10. What could be a more beautiful tree for towns and farms than a **dwarf crepe myrtle**? Crepe myrtles (*Lagerstroemia*) are especially popular full-size ornamental trees because they bloom like crazy in mid-to-late summer and have incredibly brilliant fall foliage. During the winter, when most trees are rather plain, myrtles show off their exotic peeling trunks.

Highly recommended is 'Chickasaw', with tiny leaves (½" long) that turn a bronze-red in fall. Chickasaw also has a compact growth habit, naturally growing to less than 2 feet tall. Crepe myrtles generally are hardy in Zones 7-9, but Chickasaw is reported to be fully root hardy in Zone 6, and occasionally stem hardy if well mulched for winter.

Old friends Joe and Fred spar in their weekly checkers match under the new spring foliage of the Chickasaw miniature crepe myrtle tree. It's extremely slow growing and deciduous. Photo by Sue Piper

If you can't find these miniature trees outdoors at your local nursery, try the bonsai department. Most of these trees are also available online from specialty miniature-plant growers.

—Pat Hayward

The kindest cuts

I learned the scientific theories of pruning in a college class called "Landscape maintenance techniques," but I learned the art of pruning from Larry Watson, a nurseryman I worked for, who'd been pruning trees for more than half his life. About once a month, he'd take a group of us out to the fields, choosing a different type of tree each time. We'd talk about how each species of tree grew naturally and then discuss its response to pruning. After demonstrating on a couple of trees, he'd let us each try our hand at it. We did this for a couple of years, learning the differences between pruning oak, maple, pine, spruce, and ash trees. Over time we were able to see the results of our efforts, learning what worked best for each tree species. Larry, like all good teachers, knew this was the best way to learn—first by understanding, next by doing, and then by observing our results.

Judicious pruning turns a miniature lemon-scented geranium into a colorful shade tree along the Rio Verde Western Railway of Larry and Tanya Rose in La Mesa, California. Photo by Pat Hayward

You don't need to go to these lengths to learn how to prune plants on your outdoor railroad, however, because pruning plants is pretty easy once you understand a few basic plant concepts. First, plants are living things and respond to pruning in fairly predictable ways. The second rule is that no matter how much you know about pruning, plants are living things and often respond to pruning in unpredictable ways. But not to worry: The two great things about pruning are that it's hard to kill a plant by pruning it (at least in moderation) and even the worst mistakes often can be corrected.

This is what happens when you cut a stem or branch of a tree. Normally, most of the plant's energy is directed to the tip of the stem (a process officially called "terminal growth"). Removing the tip (or terminal) of the branch diverts the energy back along the stem to its side ("lateral") buds. Don't worry if you can't see these side buds—they're usually either very small or invisible ("latent") to the human eye. In essence, removing the tips of branches actually creates bushier, denser plants because it redirects all the energy that would have gone to a few tip buds to the side buds instead.

Pruning also allows you to control the direction of new growth. If you've ever grown hybrid tea roses, you know that the normal rule is to keep the center of the bush relatively open to discourage insects and diseases. This is achieved by pruning to what's called an "outside bud," meaning that you need to find a bud pointing to the outside (rather than the inside) of the plant and prune the stem just above that bud. This redirects the energy to this "outside" bud, resulting in a new branch that will grow outward.

Thinning a tree or shrub to make it look more natural in the railroad landscape is a slightly different matter. As branches grow older, their

Pruning terms to remember

candle: the new growth of a pine, just before the needles elongate.

latent bud: a dormant or inactive bud, often invisible to the eye.

lateral bud: a bud growing along the side of a branch, usually at the base of a leaf or a needle.

pinching: removing unwanted, soft new growth with your fingertips.

terminal growth: the plant process in which most of the plant's energy is directed toward the (terminal) buds at the tip of a branch.

latent buds become less active and less able to kick into action when the terminal buds are removed. This explains how you can cut a larger branch all the way back to a main tree trunk and not end up with a mass of new growth at the pruning site, although this does happen on occasion.

Pruning conifers is a bit more complicated than pruning deciduous shrubs. Spruce trees, such as Alberta spruce, are generally easy to shape through pruning because they have very active lateral buds. *Chamaecyparis* (false cypress), junipers, and yews also have active lateral buds.

Pines react differently to pruning because their buds are much less active than those of spruce. In fact, once the needles have dropped from a pine branch, it's unlikely you'll get the tree to sprout on that branch again.

It's best to control pines when they're actively growing, at what's called the "candle" stage. A candle is the new tip growth of the pine, just before the needles start to stretch out.

If you want to control the size of a pine, simply pinch out the tip of the candle, leaving as much or as little of the new growth as you want to remain on the tree. You can even remove the entire candle if you don't want the pine to grow at all that year.

It's also better to "pinch" pine candles with your fingers instead of pruning them with cutters. Tools can injure new pine needles, which can result in burning or die-back on those needles.

Pruning is as much an art as it is a science. And, like any form of art, it takes lots of practice. Start with some inexpensive plants before you tackle bigger or more costly projects. Have specific goals in mind and experiment with different techniques. And just as professional woodworkers follow the adage "measure twice, cut once," make doubly sure to remove only the branches you mean to.

—*Pat Hayward*

Good-quality sharp pruners, such as these by Felco, make pruning jobs go smoothly. By setting the newly purchased plant up high, it's easier to see exactly which branches need to be trimmed. This is a dwarf yaupon holly. Photo by Pat Hayward

Pines, such as this dwarf mugo, should be "pinched" while in the springtime "candle" stage. The candles can be shortened to any desired height, and should be pinched just before the needles elongate. Photo by Pat Hayward

Pruning Q&A

Question: When's the best time to prune trees on a garden railroad?

A: Every time you make a cut on a plant, you're encouraging latent buds to grow. With that in mind, it's best not to encourage new growth in late summer or fall in areas with cold winters. Most plants can be pruned in the winter, spring, or early summer and recover nicely. If you want blossoms on your spring-blooming shrubs and trees (such as dwarf lilacs or spireas), it's best to prune them right after they bloom. If you prune spring-blooming plants in the summer, you'll likely prune off buds for next year's flowers. In warmer climates, you can prune plants almost any time they're actively growing.

Q: Every winter my Alberta spruce trees burn on the south side. Should I prune out the dead parts?

A: In some parts of the country (particularly in the Southwest, where there's bright sunshine, lots of wind, and low moisture in winter), many conifers, including Alberta spruce, will often show signs of "sunburn." It's best to wait until later in the spring to do any pruning on these trees. In many cases, the latent buds will soon leaf out and fill in the dead-looking areas. If those areas fail to leaf out, use this as an opportunity to create more open, natural-looking forest trees.

Q: What type of pruners should I use to trim my trees?

A: Any tool that you choose should be sharp—that's the first rule for making clean cuts that won't damage your plants. My advice is to buy one pair of really good pruners that you can use for all your pruning needs, from large-scale trees to normal-sized plants.

I use Felco pruners because they're high-quality tools that can be taken apart for cleaning and sharpening. Felco pruners come in several styles, including lighter-weight models, a model with rotating handles, and even a version for left-handed people. I also like the idea of just one pair of pruners to handle every job in the garden.

Baby's tears cover a steep bank on the Lake Tahoe & Truckee garden railroad of Sue and Don Watters in Los Altos, California. Like many mat-forming ground covers, baby's tears can be easily divided, creating more plants at little expense and with minimal effort. Don and Sue regularly use this dense patch as a propagation bed to fill in other areas of the railroad as needed. Photo by Pat Hayward

Multiply by dividing

Division is a propagation technique used by gardeners to increase their herbaceous, perennial, and bulbous plants (but not woody plants, like trees and shrubs). It's also used frequently to rejuvenate older plants that have gotten crowded or lost their vigor due to age. This method is one of the easiest ways to increase plants and is my favorite because it is so instantly gratifying.

Another advantage to dividing plants is that it doesn't require any special equipment other than a shovel, a knife, possibly a garden fork, and sometimes a strong back. Some plants (such as mat-forming ground covers) are easy to pop out of the ground, while others (such as older iris and daylilies) may require heavier equipment.

Division usually can be performed any time during the growing season, but it's most effective when done in the spring or late summer. Late-summer division works especially well in areas with hot summers, as it gives the plants a chance to get re-established during the cooler fall months. For many of us, early August can be an ideal time to divide and set out new plants because there's still plenty of growing time left before hard frosts hit. Just be sure to keep those new babies watered while it's hot.

One rule of thumb is to divide spring-blooming plants in late summer, and summer- and fall-blooming plants in the spring. This way you avoid interrupting a bloom cycle and are able to enjoy the show without missing an entire year.

Probably the most popular reason for dividing plants, especially ground covers, is to get more plants without more expense. Fast-growing mat-formers, such as thymes, sedums, veronicas, mosses, pussytoes, and baby's tears, are among the easiest and best candidates. Using a garden fork or spade, dig out either the entire plant or a portion of it, and set it aside. (For low-growing plants, you'll probably want to dig down about 3 inches.)

If your goal is to thin or reduce the size of the original plant, leave part of it intact and refill with good garden soil and/or compost, gently tamp it down, then water in thoroughly. The old plant soon will reclaim the spot for its own.

Bulbous spring-blooming *Iris reticulata* can be divided just before the foliage fades in early summer, or in the fall when the plants are completely dormant. Photo by Pat Hayward